7 STEPS TO BECOME A NEW YOU!

Heal a Relationship • Beat an Addiction

Overcome Depression and Anxiety

Based on a therapeutic blend of psychological-biblical principles

Mike Jones, M.A.

NEW PARADIGM MEDIA GRESHAM, OREGON

Cover design by Frank DeSantis
Editing and Interior design by Ken McFarland

Copyright © 2016 by Michael A. Jones
Printed in the United States of America
All Rights Reserved

Most Scripture quotations are taken from The Holy Bible, New Living Translation, copyright © 1996, 2004, 2007 by Tyndale House Foundation. Used by permission of Tyndale House Publishers, Inc., Carol Stream, IL 60188. All Rights Reserved.

Contents

1. The Road Not Taken 7
2. The Road I Took! 17
3. A Word About Checklists 25
4. Dying to live 35
5. The Become-a-New-You Protocol 41
6. Now What? 49
7. Transform Your Life With an
   Attitude of Gratitude 51
8. Ransomed! 61
9. How to Experience God and
   Become a New You! 71
10. How to Know You're Going to Heaven 79

Dedication

I am dedicating this little book to anyone willing to experiment with the simple methods presented in these pages for becoming a happier and more fulfilled human being.

You may also want to use the space below to write a personal note to anyone you're gifting with this book.

TO: _____

FROM: _____

DATE: _____

About This Book
(7 Steps to Become a New You)

I have written this book to help you be okay when most people wouldn't be. To be okay when challenges such as these (circle those that apply or add your own) are going on in your life:

- You've just been terminated from your job without cause. You're in shock, and at your age, you're unlikely to get rehired elsewhere.
- Your child is sick...again, or perhaps this time it's you...again
- Someone hit your car in a parking lot and didn't leave a note.
- Your unemployed, drug-using kid wants to move back in.
- Your significant other criticizes you because you always...
- You're in pain most of the time, and you're the only in your 30s.
- You're depressed and can't seem to snap out of it.
- Someone close to you is ill or is about to die.
- You are scheduled for an exploratory surgery and

feeling anxious

- Your unemployment is about to run out, and you have no idea how you're going to pay your rent or mortgage when it does.
- You're going through a devastating loss.

If you're not on this list, you could probably write your own. Bad things happen to all of us on this planet. That's the norm here.

But what's not normal is to be all right when everything seems to be going all wrong.

The purpose of this book is to show you how you can be okay when most folks wouldn't be. To survive life's more severe challenges, I believe we have to do something hugely radical—and that's get replaced. In other words, like a caterpillar becoming a butterfly, you must become a new you.

This book will show you how to do this. I hope you'll go for it.

"The Holy Spirit will change you into a different person."
—I Samuel 10:6

ONE

THE ROAD NOT TAKEN

HOW I BECAME A NEW ME

It was the best of times and the worst of times for me, when at the age of 27, I hooked up with Worthington Foods, a food company in the outskirts of Columbus, Ohio.

▶ It was the best of times because I arrived at a pivotal time in the life of this company and in my own professional life. I was the advertising guy. I had a vision for expanding the company's veggie meatless meats beyond the specialty food stores where they were, and into the nation's supermarkets—and we did it!

▶ But it was also the worst of times for me personally because while I believed in God, I certainly didn't know Him, my marriage wasn't working, I was addicted to my job and to cigarettes, and my wife and I were each involved in extramarital affairs.

I had two special moments at Worthington Foods. Both

occurred in 1969. The first involved a decision that resulted in my quitting smoking. The second revolved around launch of a veggie-turkey product called Holiday Roast. It was late summer of 1969 when the company made its decision to put Holiday Roast into production. However, I requested that management allow me to delay introducing that product until late October or early November because I thought an announcement a few weeks prior to Thanksgiving might be really good timing for introducing a veggie turkey to the world.

So I scheduled a press conference at the Americana Hotel in New York City. I'm pretty sure you couldn't do today what we did back then. We had a live turkey tethered to a table with an "I-Love-Worthington-Foods" sign around its neck and food for him to peck away at. Nearby, we featured veggie-turkey slices, alongside real turkey slices for a head-to-head competition.

The taste test wasn't much of a contest. The real turkey beat the veggie turkey feathers down. But that didn't matter. The media came out in droves. More than 50 reporters showed up, including the wire services, TV stations, all of the New York City newspapers, and many popular magazines of that time including *The Saturday Evening Post* and *Readers Digest.* Later we even got on The Today Show.

The resulting publicity that the meatless meats were coming to America's dinner tables went everywhere. It was a marketing guy's dream, and it put Worthington Foods on the radar of corporate America, especially companies looking to make acquisitions. I don't remember all of the corporations that came calling during the next few months, but there were many, including Coca-Cola and Miles Laboratories.

Miles Laboratories, the Alka-Seltzer people, won the competition, and that spun me into a crisis, because Miles offered me a job.

Why was a terrific job offer a crisis? Well, it was a crisis for me because earlier that year I had committed my life to God and now had a chance to earn some serious money. So why not accept the job offer as a blessing from Above? Well, perhaps in part because my Christian mentor, a New York City businessman named Emilio Knechtle, was arguing against my doing so.

"Don't go to Miles," he said. "You'll be working seven days a week. You won't have any time for God or for your family. Taking this job could well cost you your soul and your marriage."

After praying over the matter, I decided if I wanted to stay on the new road I was on, I'd better not accept the offer.

Worthington Foods president, Jim Hagle, was stunned when I told him I was going to turn down the job. He said, "At least do Miles the courtesy of flying up there and listening to them." So I did.

Miles sent down a private plane, and off I flew to Miles' corporate headquarters in Chicago, where I was wined and dined. Now my crisis was hard upon me because I could see this really was a great job opportunity. If I accepted the job, I would be the guy spearheading the vegetable-protein foods into the nation's supermarkets.

When I told Jim Hagle I was still going to turn down the offer, he told me, "Mike, you can go to Miles and not even be terribly successful and you'll still be able to call your shot almost anywhere in corporate America just having been there."

But let me give you more background on what was driving my new way of thinking. On a business trip to New York City earlier that year I had quit smoking and had begun a relationship with Jesus Christ. I came back from that trip and told the married woman I was seeing that I had made a decision for Christ.

She said, "We'll never be together again, will we?" I said,

"No, I love you too much now."

I wasn't just being glib. The sad facts were that we'd just been using each other trying to meet needs.[1] Now I was taking Jesus up on His promise to meet all of my needs. I had come to a crossroad and had made a right turn.

During my new walk with Jesus, I undertook some psychotherapy and reflected on why I had this propensity for having affairs. It finally came to me that I had been a love-starved kid who hadn't yet dealt with the baggage of a devastatingly-low self-esteem I was still carrying around from my childhood. Too often, I was trying to build my sense of self-worth in wrong places.

My mother was love starved herself, an emotionally gaping hole, some of us thought. Dad loved her dearly, but it was never enough. So she didn't have much love for him or for me. She used to tell me when I was 8 or 9 how much better her life with my dad was before I came along.

I don't recall receiving a lot of affirmation from my parents. When they dropped me off for my first year away at college at age 17, Mother looked at me out of her car window and said, "We don't know why we brought you down here. We know you're probably going to flunk out."

So much for some warm words of encouragement or a hug goodbye. Outraged, I simply said, "Thanks a lot, Mother," picked up my last two suitcases, and walked away with a forgiveness issue that would last until I was 30.

I was terrified for the next four years that I might flunk out—but I didn't. In fact, just to show Mother I really wasn't a loser, I went on to earn a Master's degree in journalism

---

1. God promises to meet all the needs of those who trust Him. "And my God will supply every need of yours, according to His riches in glory in Christ Jesus"—Philippians 4:19.

from American University in Washington, D.C. I was still an emotionally-needy young guy, but now I was an educated emotionally-needy young guy.

A few months after I turned down the opportunity to go to Miles Laboratories, the president of my alma mater called and invited me to teach journalism classes there.

Emilio thought I should go. I prayed about it and ultimately accepted the invitation. During the next ten years, my career path included a teaching stint at Andrews University in Southwest Michigan, the editorship of a young-adult Christian magazine called *Insight* in Washington, D.C., and then I became a pastor in Portland, Oregon, and Anchorage, Alaska.

After that, my marriage fell apart, and my wife and I divorced. I left the denomination I'd been affiliated with and also the pastoral ministry.

I was unchurched and single for the next thirteen years, during which time I founded a dental-referral business. Then I met Diane out country-western dancing and asked her for a date. But she told me she was a Christian and didn't want to risk getting involved with a guy who wouldn't go to church with her, since I had told her I was unchurched. I told Diane that church attendance was negotiable as long as she'd still dance with me. Six months later we married. As you'd expect, we attend church pretty regularly.

But the most important thing I want to share with you here is what I learned about Christianity when I came back to the church. You see, I had a stunning "aha" moment that was an absolute game changer. This happened after I read the Bible story about the prophet Samuel telling young Saul just before he became ancient Israel's first king, "The Holy Spirit will come upon you in power...and you will be changed into a different person"—1 Samuel 10:6.

What was so amazing about this insight was that I

finally began to realize I didn't just need Jesus to *forgive* me for my selfish and wrongful behavior along the way, I also needed Him to *replace* me. To be sure you understand, let me make it clear that I'm talking about a change of nature so profound that it includes metamorphosing into a completely different person.[2]

Most people don't get this. Bottom line: This experience is akin to a caterpillar going into a chrysalis, dying, and coming out a butterfly. I finally caught on that I needed that kind of experience spiritually, and I began to see that this included more than my acceptance of Jesus' dying for my sins. I was beginning to understand that I had some dying to do myself if the transformation I desperately needed was really going to happen.

Again, just to be sure you understand, please read the next sentence slowly: *This is not about a change of behavior, it's about a change of being!* That's what this book is about.

It is my considered opinion that most Christian churches, including my own, do not emphasize this. And for sure, most don't teach that I must renew this experience daily or I will go back to being me.[3]

Perhaps this is why Jesus said, "If anyone wants to follow

---

[2] I finally understood that I needed to experience the words of the old prophet Samuel when he told young Saul, "The Holy Spirit will come upon you...and you will be changed into a different person"—1 Samuel 10:6. And I needed this experience daily.

[3] George Barna of the Barna Group www.barna.org, has reported for years the devastating fact that the behavior of most professing Christians is no different from the behavior of those who make no profession of Christianity. This may be attributable to the fact that 90% of Christians do not have a biblical world view, says Barna.

Me, let him deny himself and take up his cross daily and follow Me."—Luke 9:23. The cross is where you go to die—*die to your natural self*—so there's room for a new you to emerge.[4]

Why did I need Jesus to replace me? Because, for one thing, for forty-plus years I had a counterfeit god in my life. Whenever this god showed up, I fell on my face and worshipped even though I often tried not to. I usually asked for forgiveness, but after a while even that became too embarrassing. So I would just get high, then crash and burn whenever the temptation came at me, and sink into depression afterward.

My false god was a compulsion, an addiction. It was really intoxicating. I had a terribly unwell fantasy life. I was spiritually ill, and I would contend mentally ill as well. This counterfeit god gave me such an amazing high that I was usually unable to resist even when I realized it was killing me. It was like falling into a fast-moving river and not being able to get out.

Speaking of rivers, on June 30, 2011, I fell into the John Day River in central Oregon. I was catapulted out of a raft while with my son, Pat, who was visiting from Texas. Seconds after I hit the water, I found myself in a bone-chilling current so cold that a search-and-rescue person told me a week later when I came back for my raft and fishing gear that if I had been in that river for ten minutes, I would have died.

No one was around to help me when I fell in. All Pat

---

[4] Why do I need a new self? Because the Bible says, "*The (natural) heart is deceitful above all things and desperately corrupt; who can understand it?*"—Jeremiah 17:9. In our natural state, we're a mess. Psychiatrist M. Scott Peck writes in *The Road Less Traveled* that *most of us are mentally ill, just to different degrees.*

could do was watch and pray as I was swept away. After being expelled from my raft, I was immediately sucked into nearly 100 yards of forty-degree white water. I was dragged to the bottom at least three times as the river wrenched my body through the violent rapids. My life jacket was just a small nuisance to the river as it had its way with me.

Each time I fought to the surface, my lungs about to burst, all I had time for was one gulp of air and then I was sucked under again. Did I pray? you might ask. You bet I prayed. As I recall, about six words as I went into the maelstrom: "Jesus, please. Not here, not now." I felt sure I was going to die. Then the river took over, flinging my body around like a dishrag. It was a nightmare.

My son Pat could do nothing except watch in horror and pray from the safety of the raft that somehow I would survive. My situation was complicated by the fact that once I was out of the white water, the current took me to the middle of the river and held me there as it swept me at least a quarter of a mile downstream and out of his sight.

Hypothermia began setting in quickly.

After six or seven minutes, I was so cold and so exhausted that I couldn't swim any more. I was in the river close to eight minutes. Toward the end I could feel my life literally draining out of me. I was nearing the end of my tether, when all at once the current swept me from the middle of the river close to one of the banks.

At the same time, some small bushes growing at the water's edge came into view. I made a desperate lunge in an attempt to grab a handful, then held on for dear life. The fast-moving current tried to pull me back in. But in my struggle to survive, and exerting every ounce of strength in my wasted body, I slowly inched myself out of the river, ending up face down on the bank with my chest heaving.

I'll finish the story in the next chapter.

"The Holy Spirit will change you into a different person."
—*I Samuel 10:6*

TWO

THE ROAD I TOOK!

HOW YOU CAN BECOME A NEW YOU

Pat found me about a half mile downstream, really messed up. I was holding onto a large rock, still gasping for air. I wasn't able to respond to any of his questions. He said I was white as a sheet. But I was alive!

He fished the car keys out of my sodden jeans, scrambled up a steep thirty-foot embankment, and came back a few minutes later with our car. Picture Pat pushing/pulling/tugging a tottering me slowly up that steep, rock-strewn bank, calling out encouragement every few feet when I had to stop. "Come on, Dad, you can do this! Give me everything you've got."

As a cop, he's seen his share of emergencies, but I'm not sure he's ever driven much faster than he did that day. As we sped toward the tiny town of Spray (population 154), only to find no medical help there, I had a splitting headache, so Pat purchased a bottle of water and also a container of aspirin. Then we began a forty-five-minute ride to the small town of Fossil to a medical facility there.

Nearly an hour after I came out of the river, my temperature in the Fossil ER was only 96 degrees. I was still shaking, but I was now able to speak. The medical personnel there helped me undress and wrapped me in blankets, then gave me more blankets. Even though the temperature outside was in the 80s, I was still shivering. Finally, after checking and rechecking my vitals, they released me, and Pat and I began the three-hour drive back to Gresham as I slowly came back to life.

I tell you this story to help you understand how for forty years a false god had me trapped in a different kind of river—a river of death whose current I had no ability to resist.

Pastor Tim Keller, in his book *Counterfeit Gods*, writes that "a counterfeit god is anything so central to your life that should you lose it, your life would hardly feel worth living." That's the way I was feeling about my addiction. Perhaps you can identify with me.

At any rate, I'd like to add this important point: *A counterfeit god can give you an amazing high. But it can never satisfy. Only your Creator God can do that.* In fact, He promises, "Take delight in the Lord, and He will give you the desires of your heart"—Psalms 37:4. Counterfeit gods, on the other hand, are just pretenders. They intoxicate even as they're killing you—and they don't care if you're high when you die.

A counterfeit god can be anything you worship: a significant other, a child, food or drink, money, your job or one you're after, a hobby or a habit. Some even worship themselves. I challenge you to ask yourself if you have any false gods in your life.

A friend of mine died recently of cirrhosis of the liver.

After years of alcohol worship, she gave up her false god, but only after that god had signed her death warrant. Worshiping a false god always kills, albeit slowly. Hers was a long and painful death. It took her nearly a year to die.

Keller writes, "In ancient times, the false gods were bloodthirsty. They still are."

So what are we to do about our counterfeit gods? Whether yours is a compulsion to be CEO or a substance addiction, it's virtually impossible to stop worshiping a counterfeit god without dying yourself. This isn't a physical death. It's a daily dying to the nature you were born with. Why daily? Because your old nature won't stay dead even after you think you've killed it. Like the evil robot in Arnold Schwarzenegger's "Terminator 2" movie, it's always trying for a comeback. That's the nature of the beast.

In the right side of my brain (the feeling side), I felt like my life wouldn't be worth living if I gave up my counterfeit god, such was its grip on me.

I have come to believe that the highs our counterfeit gods can generate are so intoxicating because they are often demonically enhanced. Think about this as you ask yourself if you have any false gods in your life. The Israelites of old must have been in some kind of demonic overwhelm that they could plunge knives into their babies' chests and sacrifice them to Baal, the sun god they were worshiping back then. I can't fathom that,[5] although the Bible is clear that it happened.

Some still sacrifice their offspring today. They rarely see them because they're worshiping some false god—often their work or their career climb. Others sacrifice their children by worshiping the kids themselves. The kids can

---

5. "They have filled this place with the blood of innocent children. They have built pagan shrines to Baal, and there they burn their sons as sacrifices to Baal."—Jeremiah 19:4, 5.

20 • 7 STEPS TO BECOME A NEW YOU!

do no wrong, but when they fall off the precarious pedestals their parents have them on, as they always will in time, the parents are done with them.

It's embarrassing to admit that giving up my false god (in my case, a corrupted fantasy life)[6] was one of the most difficult decisions I've ever had to make. As you'd expect, the devil counterattacked even while I was deciding. And he told me at some level, "You give this up, and you'll be a Christian all right, Jones. And the rest of your stupid life will be one holy bore. You will become a nuh, spelled N-U-H—nuh."

That was a lie. Not that I haven't had my challenges, and the devil still takes his shots at me. But even when I slip, I have promises such as this one to get me through: "The righteous [person] falls seven times and rises again..."—Proverbs 24:16. Isn't that an amazing promise? Still accounted righteous after we've fallen. I claim it often.

My life for the last fifteen years has been largely one of love, joy, and deep satisfaction despite the turbulence of living on this planet. I am married to a woman who loves me. We don't have unlimited funds, but Diane and I have enough. In recent years, we've even been able to travel to Paris, London, Rome, and some of the Bible lands. We don't have homes in these places but we do have one in Heaven fully paid for, thanks to Jesus.[7] We believe we'll see Him soon!

As I mentioned in the previous chapter, my breakthrough came when I had an epiphany while reading a Bible story. Young Saul was about to become ancient Is-

---

6 Counterfeit gods can be so-called "good" things, too. Though I didn't say so in chapter 1, my compulsion for career success was certainly a false god for me when I was in my twenties.

7. "In my father's house are many mansions... I go to prepare a place for you. When everything is ready, I will come and get you, so that you will always be with me."—John 14:2-3, KJV; NLT

rael's first king, and the prophet Samuel told him, "The Holy Spirit will come upon you in power...and you will be changed into a new person."—1 Samuel 10:6. When I read that, I suddenly realized, "This thing has had me for forty years, and I'm not beating it. I am going to have to become a different person if I'm going to get better."

In other words, I needed a new self. This meant that the original me had to go in order to make room for a new me. I recognized that only the Spirit of God could do something that profound. And so in the minutes that followed as I made the choice to give up my false god, I prayed something close to these words out loud, "Lord, please change me into a different person!"

Choosing is everything!

Why is choosing so important? Because in our own strength, few of us can give up our false gods by ourselves when we exercise our power of choice—even in the face of overwhelming feelings to the contrary—we are putting our will into action. That's when the Holy Spirit's power gets unleashed in our lives—when we give Him control of our will. Then we can begin to receive God's promises and the satisfaction He offers when we choose Him.

For example, Jesus promises, "Nothing will be impossible to you." "Behold, I give you power... over all the power of the enemy." "I will never leave you nor forsake you."—Matthew 17:20; Luke 10:19; Hebrews 13:5. Now, of course, these are just words on a page until you start claiming them. Claim them in the name of Jesus Christ, which is where they come from, and they will become a reality in your life experience.

Now who's the enemy I'm talking about? The enemy is not only the devil who is always looking for someone to

22 • 7 STEPS TO BECOME A NEW YOU!

destroy,[8] it is also us. In our natural state, you and I are our own worst enemy. Apart from being emptied of self every day, human nature is ever ready for negative expression, eager for a scrap, or ready to indulge being hurt. Even hugely successful people go sideways (think Martha Stewart, Lance Armstrong, Bill Cosby, Steve Jobs, Brian Williams, Gen. David Petraeus, Senators Gary Hart and John Edwards, Governor Mark Sanford, various senators and congressmen, and whoever else of prominence has crashed lately).

If you will choose to be emptied of self every day, incredible things will begin to happen. For one thing, you will become infused with all the power of the Godhead. You'll even obtain power over yourself, something almost unheard of these days! In addition, you will have an almost unbelievable satisfaction at your core that will get you through the most difficult times.

By the way, this choosing, is not one and done. Behavioral science tells us it takes about eight weeks to start a new habit.[9] So don't worry about your setbacks after you fall, as you will. Just get back up again. Don't trust your feelings. Like a basketball player on defense, the devil will be desperate to knock you off your game through the "D" words: discouragement, deception, diversion, depression, and dilemmas. Don't let him. Remember, you are on the

---

8. See "The Devil Made Me Do It" in my book, *Snakebit: we're all snakebit*, for a biblical depiction of the war between Christ and Satan, who is an actual fallen angel turned demon. Available at Amazon.com
9. "How Long Does It Take To Form A New Habit," Huffington Post, Healthy Living, April 10, 2014

road to awesome.

Awesome Joy!

Awesome Power!

Awesome Satisfaction at your core!

It's my purpose in this book to help you acquire that power and that joy! But obtaining it will require that you acquire a new core every day. Most folks aren't willing to pay the dying-to-self price. For me, this calls for a time commitment of at least thirty minutes first thing every day with God. While you're thinking about that, I'll share next how a checklist can be a game changer if you will adopt one and follow it relentlessly every day.

"The Holy Spirit will change you into a different person."
—*I Samuel 10:6*

THREE

A WORD ABOUT CHECKLISTS

On Oct. 30, 1935, the U.S. Army Air Corps held a flight competition for airplane manufacturers seeking to build a new generation of long-range bombers. The competitors were Martin & Douglas and Boeing.

Boeing was expected to win because its bomber could carry five times as many bombs, fly faster, and twice as far as previous bombers. But when the Boeing plane took off, it climbed to 300 feet, stalled, turned on one wing and crashed killing the pilot and two crew members.

What had gone wrong? The pilot had forgotten to release a new locking mechanism on the elevator and rudder controls. "Too much airplane for one man to fly" was the verdict. Douglas' was declared the winner and Boeing nearly went bankrupt.

Afterward, a group of test pilots met to reflect on the problem, and they came up with an ingeniously simple solution: they created a pilot checklist, perhaps one of the first checklists ever. This checklist was simple, brief, and small enough to fit on an index card.

Using this checklist, pilots went on to fly this airplane 1.8 million miles without one accident. This was the plane that gave the military a decisive advantage over the Nazis in World War 2 and helped defeat them. That plane is remembered today as the famous B-17.

In *The Checklist Manifesto,* Dr. Atul Gawande, a surgeon who leads the World Health Organization's *Safe Surgeries Saves Lives* program, writes about what he calls the *dumb* checklist. He uses the word *dumb* because checklists simply state the obvious about such basics as physicians washing their hands and wearing a mask before performing surgeries to pilots setting the flaps and doing the other essentials they all know before taking off.

Today, most surgeons and virtually all pilots use checklists to help them carry out their duties successfully.

A checklist is simply a series of five to seven steps for doing something. It should fit on a 3" by 5" index card. Why have a checklist? Because we live in a world today that is more complex because of too much information (TMI). Bottom line: if you don't get the knowledge right, you might lose the patient or the airplane. Or have something else go wrong.

Since Dr. Gawande was leading the way for checklists to be used in surgeries in the world's hospitals, he began using them in his own surgeries. Not because he needed them, he writes, but because, as he put it, he didn't want to be perceived as a hypocrite.

He writes in his book, "*In my heart of hearts, if you had strapped me down and threatened to take out my appendix without anesthetic unless I told the truth, did I think the checklist would make much difference in my cases? In my cases? Please!*"

Then he goes on to report, "*To my chagrin, however, I have yet to go through a week in surgery without the checklist's leading us to catch something we would have missed.*

Take last week as I write this, we had three catches in five cases."

One of the first known surgical checklists was created in 2001 by a critical-care specialist at John Hopkins Hospital to help prevent central line infections in patients. The result? After one year, the central line infection rate fell from 11 percent to zero. Over two years, the use of a checklist prevented an estimated 43 infections and eight deaths at the hospital.

Checklists have made their way into the world's operatories in recent years, saving millions of dollars in extended patient care and saving thousands of lives. Here's an example my doctor used before performing a cataract surgery on my right eye a few months ago. He and his surgical team went through each of these steps in advance of the surgery:

Name of Patient
Date of Birth
Which Eye (R or L)
Lens Implant Model & Power
Any Patient Allergies
Any other Considerations

Since I was awake for this surgery, I was comforted as I listened to him process this checklist with me and with the other members of his team. At least I knew they had the right eye.

My own challenges in life are what led me to create my own checklist. It has served me wonderfully in skirting the potholes we all encounter on our journeys. I hope you will consider developing a checklist of your own in the near future. Here's mine with some explanation.

CHECKLIST TO A NEW YOU

Because our world is a war zone, I always start my

day by following this seven-point checklist.[10] For me, my checklist is not just important, it is essential. I use it to get replaced with a new me every morning, and you can too. I've entitled it "My Daily Metamorphosis" so I can remember its purpose—to help me achieve transformation. Scan it now. I'll take you through it shortly in greater detail.[11]

Checklist to a New You– My Daily Metamorphosis

1. Invite God into your life, seek the Holy Spirit's infilling, surrender your will to God's will

2. Ask for a new heart and for the mind of Christ. (This means seeking a spiritual heart transplant & the mind of Christ every day.)

3. Go to the Cross in your imagination, look at Jesus, and die to self. (Amazing transformation will begin as you do this every day.)

4. Ask God to change you into a different person—1 Samuel 10:6.

5. "Eat" Jesus' flesh & blood (claim His promises) per John 6:53, 63.

6. Put on the whole armor of God—Ephesians 6:14-17.

7. Ask God to show you who He wants to love today through you.

The reason for the first six points is to get you to the sev-

---

10. I got the idea for a checklist from Atul Gawande's *The Checklist Manifesto* (Henry Holt & Co., 2009, New York, NY) in which he describes how a simple checklist now used in most surgeries has saved thousands of lives in recent years.

11. An expanded view of this checklist entitled "The Becoming A New You Protocol" can be found next in the "Dying to Live" chapter. However, I use this shorter version early every morning without exception.

A Word About Checklists • 29

enth point, a wonderful ideal for your life. But first, a quick word about the term metamorphosis, which is really what my checklist is all about.

The dictionary defines metamorphosis as "the process of transformation from an immature form to an adult form in two or more distinct stages."[12] That's the primary purpose of my checklist: To enable me, or whoever is following it, to go from caterpillar to butterfly in terms of our journey. To go from an immature being to one who is mature.

This transformation is so dramatic that I will try to illustrate the change by sharing how caterpillars become butterflies.

During its first two weeks of life, a caterpillar eats 3,000 times its weight, then spins a chrysalis around itself and dies. During the next 10 days a fascinating process takes place that results in the total death of the caterpillar and the birth of a very different creature—a butterfly.

As you know, these two creatures are totally different in every way.

- ▸ The caterpillar can only crawl, whereas the butterfly can fly, some for very long distances.
- ▸ The caterpillar's eye can only see light, while the butterfly's eye can see multiple colors.
- ▸ The butterfly's four wings have thousands of microscopic scales much like the space shuttle tiles.
- ▸ Monarch butterflies can fly for thousands of miles, while the caterpillar rarely leaves the plant where it was hatched.

Yes, the butterfly is a totally different creature. You will be, too, if you follow your checklist relentlessly.

To help illustrate the point further, take a good look at the Bible's description of the Natural Self you were born

---
12. *The Random House College Dictionary*, Revised Edition, 1984, by Random House, Inc., New York, NY

with, then the Supernatural Self God wants to give you afresh every day. Examine each table that follows carefully and know that even if you only have few of the negative points listed under the Natural Self (let's say you tell white lies once in a while or can be Judgmental or Mean), don't you think those are inappropriate for someone who's enroute (if you're a Bible Christian) to becoming one of God's ambassadors to the Universe?[13]

Fact is, if you go for the Supernatural Self experience every day with the help of your checklist, you will begin to acquire its characteristics and those of your new Best Friend. Also, over time, the negative characteristics of your Birth Self will be squeezed out of your life.

On that point, Jesus says our highest purpose is to love God supremely and those around us as much as we love ourselves.[14] You can demo godly love in many ways. Donating a kidney to someone who needs one is one way. But so is making eye contact and smiling at a stranger. Also, in our isolated world, human touch can be quite wonderful. For instance, even a pat on the arm, a gentle touch on the shoulder.

Once I put my hand on the shoulder of an older woman in my church. She quickly pulled my hand away and said, "That's my bad shoulder." I apologized and observed that Jesus tended to touch people a lot and they seemed to feel better afterward. She immediately put my hand back on her shoulder.

Many ways exist to love our neighbors, and even the tiniest can be significant. But as you look at the two tables which follow,[15] it's clear that the Supernatural Self table is where you want to end up.

---

13. Of the faithful servant, Jesus says, "He will put him in charge of all His possessions."—Luke 12:44, NIV
14. "I am giving you a new commandment: Love each other."—John 13:34
15. These are my compilation of the Bible's primary descriptions of our two natures.

NATURAL SELF	SUPERNATURAL SELF
Galatians 5:19-21; Ephesians 5:17-19	Galatians 5:22, 23; Ephesians 4:22-24
Caterpillar Person Characteristics	*Butterfly Person Characteristics*
Proud & Self Serving	Loves Everyone
Unhappy/Depressed	Serves Others
Ambitious to a fault	Joyful & Steady
Impatient/Unkind	Humble, Not Proud
Deceitful & Rebellious	Kind & Encouraging
Corrupted Thinking	Open and Meek
Overly Sensitive	Good Thoughts
Fearful/ Anxious	Gentle Yet Powerful
Contentious & Needy	Self-Controlled
Hard-Hearted/Mean	Pure & Moral
Dishonest & Immoral	Generous/Sweet
Dark & Paranoid	No Fear/No Anxiety
Envious & Jealous	Meek & Humble
Critical/Unforgiving	Forgiving/No Grudges
Addictive Tendencies	Enlightened & Wise
My Need to Be Right	Happy & Fulfilled
Rarely Satisfied	You Might Be Right
It's All About Me	It's All About God & You

To be totally candid with you, when I looked carefully at the Natural Self table, I had more than just Corrupted Thinking to deal with. I admit to at least eight negative characteristics. So don't feel like the Lone Ranger that you have your own assortment. We all do.

But now here's the point. Follow your checklist every

day and you'll never have to go back to being a caterpillar person, spiritually shallow, more afraid of God than comfortable with Him. In this life, we all start out as caterpillars desperately in need of becoming butterflies.

So, anyway, you and I don't want to remain caterpillar people. We want to become butterfly people—positive difference makers in the lives of those around us, our own lives full of love, joy, peace, and power. Butterfly people are the ones Jesus instructs "to heal the sick, raise the dead, cleanse lepers, and cast out demons."[16] And help take the good news about His soon return to the entire world. You okay with that?[17]

I trust now that you can understand why the checklist you're receiving here comes packaged with the goal of transformation. If you follow the Creator God of the Bible, you have an exciting future ahead of you. So why not use your checklist every day and become transformed every day!

Please look at the checklist again and take a minute to read the steps. Second, practice talking your way through each point out loud. (This will take a little longer. It takes me thirty minutes or more.) Third, watch what happens after just one week as you incorporate the checklist into your life first thing every morning. Stick with this for eight weeks,[18] and I am confident you will be able to see the Holy Spirit transforming you into a new person.

P.S. When I take thirty minutes or more on a daily basis with my checklist—and I admit sometimes in the early morning I'm slow getting out of the gate—a momentum kicks in. I become a different person capable of getting through the mine field of the day ahead no matter what

---

16 Matthew 10:8.
17 I am coming soon, and my reward is with me to give everyone according as his work shall be."—Revelation 22:12
18 That's how long behavioral scientists now believe it takes to start a new habit and have it stick.

the demons throw at me. One reason for this is I start walking with God in the here and now every day. And this gets wonderfully personal, even impacting how I handle my phone calls and how I think.

To encourage you, allow me to share with you how with the help of this simple checklist, God is transforming my life. To do this, I will list eight characteristics from the Natural Self chart that were alive and well in my life when I began asking God to replace me a few years back.

Needy	Selfishly Ambitious
Overly Sensitive	Critical & Negative
Corrupted Thinking	Addicted
Impatient	Rebellious

Thanks to God's work in my life, today most of these characteristics are greatly diminished, and some are gone. They are being replaced by the wonderfully-different characteristics of my new self. Sure, the old self shows up from time to time, but when it does, the Lord encourages me with promises such as this one as He continues to defeat the negatives in my life:

"And I am sure that God, Who began the good work within you, will continue His work until it is finally finished on that day when Christ Jesus comes back again."—Philippians 1:6 NLT

I don't want to suggest to you that I've arrived. I've really only just begun. I do understand I can't earn my salvation. It's simply a gift I receive when I receive Jesus as Savior and Lord, something I do daily. Any good behavior on my part is simply the result of having Jesus in my life. As I continue to receive Him every day, the characteristics of His nature are beginning to replace the negative traits of my old self.

Here to encourage you on your journey are a few of the more positive traits that are emerging in my life as I continue to go through my daily checklist/metamorphosis:

More Loving	Less Anxiety/Fear
More at Peace	More Self-Control
Increased Patience	Increased Wisdom
More Forgiving	More Addiction Free

I hope you get the idea. As you process your checklist every morning, the Holy Spirit will replace the old you with the new you. This allows God to continue to replace your negative characteristics with the fruit of His Spirit which indwells you. This is a wonderfully satisfying way to live. It's the only sensible way to live.

You will recall that when my son, Pat, found me after my escape from the John Day River, I was holding onto a large rock. Perhaps you're seeking to escape from some river of death yourself (maybe a counterfeit god—some addiction or ugly character trait that has you trapped—or maybe you're just needing to get away from you). If so, may I suggest that employing a checklist might be just the ticket to get you connected to the Rock Christ Jesus and then get propelled into a very different kind of river.

The Bible calls this, "the river of God's delight."

So think of your checklist as a river. A river that will transform you into a new you.

I hope you'll take the plunge![19]

---

19 Psalm 36:8

"The Holy Spirit will change you into a different person."
—*I Samuel 10:6*

FOUR

DYING TO LIVE

The protocol which follows is my attempt to explain more fully the small checklist in the previous chapter. It is based on my belief in the Creator-God of the Bible and on certain psychological principles[20] such as cognitive therapy.

Now you may not believe as I do. Your belief might be based on a higher power, but you're not sure about who or what that power is—or you may not believe in much of anything.

Just know this: You don't need to be in lockstep with me in order for these points to help you. You need only to be willing to experiment that the Creator-God might be working in your life. After all, He does invite you to "taste

---

20. Carol Dweck's wonderful book, *Mindset: the new psychology of success,* Ballantine Books, 2008; describes the incredible value of having a growth mindset if one is to continue to grow in life.

and see that the Lord is good"—Psalms 34:8. So what have you got to lose if you give God a taste test when He invites you to do just that?

But first, let me reiterate that the Creator-God's purpose for our lives is that we should be beautiful people—kind, unselfish, patient, gracious, and loving—not mean or critical. Instead, easy to be with—beautiful on the inside no matter what we look like on the outside—and handling life's stressors with serenity.

The Bible says we can do that this way: "Put off your old self, which is being corrupted by its deceitful desires...and put on the new self, created to be like God"—Ephesians 4:22-24.

Isn't it interesting that if we permit it to have life, the natural self is always in a state of being corrupted? And the new self, which we need to put on every day, has as its highest purpose that we become like God. And it is always propelling us upward.

As we've already seen, the Bible tells us that Jesus is this kind of amazing being Who can "fill the whole universe" but can also make Himself small enough to be "at home in your heart"—Ephesians 4:10; 3:17. I share this information so you can consider that He might really be capable of changing you into a beautiful person who's at peace with God and with yourself no matter what challenges you are facing.

Your biggest issues are likely to be your ego and admitting that you really can't fix yourself—or you may lack faith that God is willing to do this for you. These are everyone's issues, and that includes those who are highly successful and feel like they really have it together.

Just know that you're safe with this Power. After all, the Bible says this is your Creator and that He died for you. So experiment with the steps that follow, and watch Him change you into an exciting new you![21] Perhaps a more humble you if you're already at the top. Or a more successful you if you feel like you're a bottom feeder just now. Because, you see, in Christ, even losers can become winners. Perhaps the following story will help illustrate the point.

Though he's no loser, my friend, Gary, a businessman in his early 70s, found himself in a biker bar a few years ago after a friend asked him to fill in for a missing player during a pool tournament. Gary isn't a biker and he's not very big. He might run 5'8" and be 165 pounds. On this occasion, a big guy who had too much to drink started challenging anyone in the bar to come out on the dance floor and fight him.

Everyone ignored him, not just because they knew he was drunk, but also because at about 6'4" and 240 pounds, taking him on would be a task few would aspire to.

However, in this instance, the guy wouldn't stop spouting. So after a few more minutes Gary got up and went over to talk with him. Picture Gary looking up at this big guy, and you'd understand why a hush fell over the bar. I mean it was just so apparent that Gary was overwhelmingly likely to be the loser if they got into it. But all Gary did was tell the big guy in a quiet voice, just above a whisper, "I think you should go home now."

Some expletives came out of the big guy's mouth, but when he pulled back his right arm to take the first swing, Gary threw up his hands and said, "Just a minute! Before you do that, you need to be sure you're really, really fast."

The big guy stopped and just looked at him in seeming

---

21. "If anyone is in Christ, he is a new creation"—2 Corinthians 5:17

disbelief. Then Gary said once again, very quietly, "I really think you should go home now."

Then, incredibly, a few seconds later, the guy turned around and walked out, and the whole bar burst into applause.

Now you may be wondering where in the world Gary found the courage to stand up to such a bully, especially at his advanced age and much smaller size. But when I tell you that Gary is not only a Christian, he also has a black belt in Taekwondo, you will be more understanding. Now you know he had an equalizer, several equalizers. I mean Jesus does tell all of His followers, "I give you power...over all the power of the enemy"—Luke 10:19.

But now what I want you to understand is this: With the use of your checklist, if you really take this seriously, you can become a different person every day and have that most fantastic of equalizers—the powers of Omnipotence—at your command. As a quick explanation, here are two promises I claim early every day so that I have them available if I get into trouble, physically or otherwise.

"If anyone lacks wisdom, let him ask God Who gives to everyone generously, and it will be given him"—James 1:5.

"The Lord will fight for you, and you have only to be still"—Exodus 14:14.

Let's say someone's out to get you at work. Perhaps you can't prove it, but you have good evidence this is happening. Why not ask God to fight for you, in harmony with the first promise! Perhaps like this: "Jesus, You said, 'Whatever you ask in My Name, I will do it, that the Father may be glorified in the Son'"—John 14:14.

"Please fight for me as You've promised, Lord. I'm claiming Your promise in the name of Jesus Christ, 'The Lord will fight for you, and you have only to be still.' Thank You for fighting for me."

Then let go of the situation. It's being handled. You no longer need to take matters into your own hands. God's promises really are your equalizer!

Once early in our marriage, Diane got after me for something I considered trivial. I told her, "I can't believe we're even having this conversation about something so petty." Diane quickly assured me we were having such a conversation. She also let me know that what I considered trivial wasn't trivial to her. (I had thrown out an old poinsettia plant which was shedding, just so you know). Anyway, suddenly it occurred to me, I wasn't going to come out well in this situation no matter how justified I felt.

So I quit trying to justify myself. Instead, I gave up on myself and began to pray silently, claiming these promises. After a few more comments, Diane fell silent, we went on to other matters, and our conflict ended.

Diane apologized the next morning for the entire incident.

So I say to you, in matters both trivial and consequential, Jesus is your equalizer and your best Friend. He promises additionally, "I will never leave you, nor forsake you. I'm with you always"—Matthew 28:20.

Now your real issue will be to see if you really believe His promises and have the faith to claim them no matter what is going on around you. The Bible assures you that "the word of God is full of living power"—Hebrews 4:12. It can transform you. It can also stop a fight and turn you into a loving human being no matter what's going on, if you're willing to exercise your faith in God's promises. Are you there yet?

"You will be changed into a different person."
—*1 Samuel 10:6*

FIVE

THE BECOME-A-NEW-YOU PROTOCOL

To get started, follow this expanded "Become-a-New-You" protocol. Think about what follows as a metaphor: a caterpillar (you) going into a chrysalis, dying, and emerging as a beautiful butterfly (a new you). These points are intended to get you into and through your own spiritual metamorphosis every day so that the Holy Spirit can enable you to (1) die to your natural corrupted self, (2) put on a new uncorrupted self, and (3) emerge transformed into an amazing supernatural being who hangs out with his or her new Best Friend every day.

Here's the promise...

"Put off your old self which is being corrupted by its deceitful desires, and put on the new self, created to be like God..."—*Ephesians 4:22-24.*

Relentlessly follow the protocol below and ingest the Scriptures in the next section daily over the next sixty days and you'll get there. By the end of the first thirty days, a new you should be emerging nicely. Please allow at least the first thirty minutes of every day for this protocol to become fully integrated into your experience.

1. **Invite God into your life every morning first thing before you do anything else.** Jesus says, "I stand at the door and knock. If anyone opens the door, I will come in"—Revelation 3:20. So invite Him in. Just say, "Lord, please come in. I welcome You into my life and ask that You transform me today into a different person."

2. **Ask God to give you a new or renewed heart and to install His mind in place of yours.** Just say, "Lord, You've promised to give me a new heart and said I can have 'the mind of Christ.' Please give me these two amazing gifts today through your indwelling Holy Spirit"—Ezekiel 36:26; 1 Corinthians 2:16.

3. **Now ask God to enable you to experience 1 Samuel 10:6: "The Spirit of the Lord will...change you into a different person."** Ask Him, "Please make these words efficacious in my life right now, I pray in Jesus' name." Remember Jesus' promise, "Whatever you ask in My Name, I will do it..."—John 14:13. You're just asking Him to do what He's promised to do.

4. **Next go to the Cross (in your mind's eye) and reflect on what Jesus did for you there.** When the Israelites of old rebelled and found themselves being bitten by deadly sand vipers and dying (Numbers 21), God told them to look at an artificial snake hanging on a pole. This didn't make any sense, but it worked. Those who looked lived, and those who didn't died. The bronze snake was a symbol of a Savior to come,

Who says to you today, "Hey, you're snakebit, too. Look to Me and be saved"—Isaiah 45:22. So spend a few minutes at the Cross, won't you? As you look to Jesus, tell Him, "In the words of the apostle Paul, I acknowledge that I've been crucified with You, and it is no longer I who live, but You Who live in me"—Galatians 2:20. Jesus spent six hours on the Cross bleeding out for you. Got just a drop of faith? Use it. Look and live!

5. **Ask God to infuse His grace into your life.** He tells us in Scripture, "My grace is sufficient for you, for My power is made perfect in weakness"— 2 Corinthians 12:9. God's transforming grace is a mysterious attribute of the Godhead which is lethal to your old nature and brings divine life to your new self. It is critical that you obtain fresh infusions of grace daily. It's perfectly okay to snack on grace throughout the day, by the way.

6. **Tell God out loud, "Thank You for transforming me into a different person."** Do you suffer from low self-esteem? It's time to start getting over that. "Those who are led by the Spirit of God are sons [and daughters] of God...heirs of God and co-heirs with Christ"—Romans 8:14, 17. Jesus has promised that one day you—yes, you—will sit with Him on His throne (Revelation 3:21) assisting in the administration of the universe.[22]

7. **Practice "eating" God's Bible promises.** The prophet Jeremiah once wrote, "When Your words came, I ate them. They were my joy and my heart's delight."—Jeremiah 15:16. Here's an example of how you can eat one of God's promises: "If anyone lacks wisdom, let him ask God Who gives everyone

---

22. God says He will put His faithful servant *"in charge of all His possessions"*—Matthew 24:47

generously, and it will be given him"—James 1:5.

Tell the Lord, "Please make this promise a reality in my life right now. Give me Your wisdom for every decision I'll make today." Do this with any of God's promises, and they are yours, as you claim them in Jesus' Name.

Now reflect on your new identity in Jesus Christ. You're royalty now! Let that fact sink in. Over time, that truth will enhance your new healthy self-esteem and help you maintain the new you! You are an ambassador-in-training of the King of the universe—a universe believed (at this writing) to include at least 100 billion galaxies, many of which you'll be visiting one of these days!

So expect intergalactic space travel, almost assuredly at the speed of thought, to be in your future as you zip through the universe on missions for God throughout eternity. Did you think you were just going to sit on a cloud and strum a harp once you got to Heaven?

When you're up to it, begin ingesting the promises on the next few pages to continue your metamorphosis into an amazing new person who's exchanged his/her old life for a new one. In the process, I assure you that you will begin to sense the presence of your new Best Friend.

Note: I don't want to push you into overwhelm. So you can pause here if you wish. But when you are ready, begin processing what's next. Don't expect some kind of rush. Just do it. Like a caterpillar spending 10 days in a cocoon, you're beginning your metamorphosis toward becoming a new being. So stay relentlessly with this dying-to-self process. You're on your way to awesome!

Some Scriptures to Ingest As You Continue Your Metamorphosis

When He had 70 disciples, Jesus told them, "Whoever eats My flesh and drinks My blood has eternal life." And 58 left Him. To the twelve who stuck around, He explained: "The flesh counts for nothing. The words I have spoken to you are spirit and they are life"—John 6:53, 63. The prophet Jeremiah once wrote, "When Your words came, I ate them"—Jeremiah 15:16. How can you "eat" God's promises? You can start by claiming them as God's gift to you and asking the Holy Spirit to implant them in your being. The result will be an amazing new you who is acquiring a personal relationship with your Creator. Here's how I do this out loud every day.

Sample Prayer and Protocol

Good morning, Father. It's [your name here] down here in the war zone of Earth and coming in the name of Jesus Christ before Your throne of grace to continue my metamorphosis into a new me. Lord, You've said in Scripture, "Fear not, for I am with you; be not dismayed, for I am your God. I will help you, I will strengthen you, I will uphold you with My victorious right hand"—Isaiah 41:10. I claim this promise for myself right now in Jesus' name.

Lord, You've also told me, "Fear not, for I have redeemed you, I have called you by name [your name here] you are Mine. When you pass through the waters, I will be with you; and through the rivers, they will not [drown] you. When you walk through the fire, you will not be burned neither will the flame kindle upon you, for I am the Lord your God, the Holy One of Israel, your Savior... and I love you"—Isaiah 43:1-3, 5.

I always tell God, "I love You back, Lord. Thanks for telling me that You love me and that I'm Yours."

You may claim any of these promises in the same way. I try to claim them all every day, asking the Holy Spirit to make them a reality in my life every day.

"It is the Lord who goes before you; He will not fail you

nor forsake you; do not fear or be dismayed"—Deuteronomy 31:8.

"The Lord says, 'I will rescue those who love Me, I will protect those who trust in My Name; when they call upon Me, I will answer. I'll be with them in trouble, I will rescue them and honor them, I will satisfy them with a long life and give them my salvation"—Psalms 91:14-16

CLAIM THESE NEW-YOU PROMISES TOO

Lord, You've also instructed:

- "Don't copy the behavior and customs of this world, but let God transform you into a new person by changing the way you think"—1 Corinthians 2:16; Romans 12:2. I choose to be out of my mind and invite You to install the mind of Christ in me so I can think correctly.

- "The Spirit of the Lord will come upon you with power...and you will be changed into a different person"—1 Samuel 10:6. Please do as You have promised, Lord, and fill me with the Holy Spirit."

- "I am your shield and your exceeding great reward."—Genesis 15:1, NIV.

- "If anyone is in Christ, he is a new creation; the old has gone, the new has come"—2 Corinthians 5:17.

INGEST THESE PROMISES ALSO

"I will never leave you nor forsake you"[23]—Hebrews 13:5

---

23. If I'm a new creation in Christ, why do I so often want to do the wrong thing? When you're *"in Christ,"* you have a new software—the mind of Christ. However, your hardware (your body and brain) will retain many of its old negative tendencies and memories until Jesus Christ returns and gives you a new body and brain. Process this protocol every day, and over time you'll find yourself doing the right thing more and more.

"*For our sake You made [Jesus] to be sin who knew no sin that in Him I might become the righteousness of God*"—2 Corinthians 5:21.

"*And to know the love of Christ, which surpasses knowledge, that [I] may be filled with all the fullness of God*"— Ephesians 3:19.

"*Don't get drunk...Instead be filled with the Holy Spirit*"— Ephesians 5:18.

"*Behold, I give you power... over all the power of the enemy*"—Luke 10:19.

"*Nothing will be impossible to you*"—Matthew 17:20.

"*I will dwell in them and walk in them, and I will be their God and they will be my people*"—2 Corinthians 6:16.

"*You will seek Me and find Me when you search for Me with all your heart. I will be found by you*"—Jeremiah 29:13.

"*I'm with you always, even to the end of the world*"—Matthew 28:20.

"Jesus, I claim each of these wonderful promises in Your name right now and look forward to Your companionship throughout this day. I choose to trust You for better or worse, no matter how my day goes."

Remember, you've been saved to serve. So go into your day now and find who God wants to love today through you.

"The Holy Spirit will change you into a different person."
—I Samuel 10:6

SIX

NOW WHAT?

You have just read the most important chapters in this book! If all you do from here on is re-read these early chapters daily, perhaps with a highlighter in hand (or using Kindle's highlighter function), know that they are calculated to help you achieve transformation in your journey and become a new you.

Beyond doing this, what I would suggest you do from here is examine the chapter headings in the remainder of this book and read those that are of greatest interest to you. Then use the early chapters as a foundation to enable you to maximize your results with these future chapters.

If you've never found Christianity to work for you before at a deep level, I am hopeful that Chapters 3 and 4 will help you get some major power in your life and give you a deeper sense of being filled with all the fullness of God.

Like those who hit the gym every day and grind out their treadmills and other protocols so they can be physically fit, be relentless in following the checklists and protocols provided here so you can stay spiritually fit. Be patient as you process your daily metamorphosis steps. I'm confident that you will enjoy your new self as it emerges and also a new and deeper friendship with Jesus that comes with it.

Keep in mind the Bible's injunction to serve others. This is your highest purpose. It is what will bring you the greatest joy and satisfaction in your life. The apostle Paul puts it this way:

"For you, dear friends, have been called to live in freedom, not freedom to satisfy your sinful nature, but freedom to serve one another in love. For the whole law can be summed up in one command, 'Love your neighbor as yourself'"—Galatians 5:13, 14.

Blessings to you on your journey.

"The Holy Spirit will change you into a different person."
—*I Samuel 10:6*

SEVEN

TRANSFORM YOUR LIFE WITH AN ATTITUDE OF GRATITUDE

So if you woke up this morning all achy and with a sore throat and fever, did you have an attitude of gratitude—or did you groan and pull the covers back over your head?

If you dragged your body to work and lamented about your affliction to a Bible-thumping co-worker, he or she might have told you to "always be thankful, for this is God's will for you..."[24] And you might have responded, "Don't beat me up with the Bible, I'm sick!"

But, hey, did you know that recent scientific studies demonstrate that those who maintain an attitude of gratitude despite their circumstances are healthier and happier than those who let negative events drag them down?

A leading scientific expert on gratitude, a psychology professor named Robert Emmons, of the University of

---
24. 1 Thessalonians 5:18

52 • 7 STEPS TO BECOME A NEW YOU!

California, reports research demonstrating that people who wrote down five things for which they were thankful were happier, healthier, less stressed, more optimistic, and more likely to help others then those who didn't have such a protocol.

Start a gratitude protocol and you can check these results out for yourself. Personally, I don't keep a journal, but recently I began verbalizing out loud every morning my appreciation of five things that I'm grateful for. It only takes about one minute, and for me it is one of the most essential minutes of my day. By the way, this exercise really does a number on depression, in case that's an issue for you.

If I were to ask you to name five things right now that you are thankful for, think you could do this in one minute? What comes to mind first? With me, I usually start by expressing appreciation that I'm still here, that I have a roof over my head, for the wellness I've enjoyed most of my life. Sometimes I just say thanks that I got my balky contact lens in on the first try instead of the twelfth. The rest comes quickly.

Debra Norville, in her book, *Thank You Power,* reports the research of two University of California professors who had three groups of volunteers focus respectively on one of three things for a week:

- difficulties in their lives
- things for which they were grateful, and
- ordinary life events which were neither negative nor positive

The group that focused on gratitude was much happier than those in the other two groups. They reported few negative physical symptoms such as headaches or colds. They spent almost an hour and a half a week more than

Transform Your Life With an Attitude of Gratitude • 53

the other groups exercising. They were less depressed, less envious, less anxious, and much more likely to reach out to help others. Having an attitude of gratitude made all the difference.

What can you and I do to develop a better attitude of gratitude? A recent issue of *Vibrant Health* magazine lists steps we can all pursue. Here are several of them, with a brief comment by me:

1. **Learn to reframe negative situations.** Dr. Emmons says, "Try this mental exercise the next time something unfortunate happens. Say to yourself, 'Yes, this is bad, but at least I _____'"—and fill in the blank.'" Sometimes Diane and I do this by saying, "At least we have a roof over our heads," or, "We still have each other," or, "We were able to pay our bills this month."

2. **Express your thanks to those around you.** Make it a point to tell the people in your life—especially those you live with—something you appreciate about them. I've told Diane along the way that I admire the fact she cares about people. I also tell her from time to time how much I appreciate the moxie she employs decorating our house, often with some pretty cool stuff from Goodwill—and not from Saks Fifth Avenue.

   You can do much the same with those in your life. Maybe even the person checking out your items at the grocery store. Once, I told a checker, "Rita, you're the best!" because she is so friendly, efficient, and fast. I was surprised at her reaction. She started crying and said, "Thank you for caring." It turned out she was dealing with some wrongful criticism from someone in management and not having a good day.

   Whenever we affirm others, we get a lift, too. Try it and see.

3. **Slow down and take time to appreciate the little things.** Author Anna Quindlan writes, "Dying people don't cling to life...to make another million or to get on [a hot TV show]. They cling to life because all of a sudden...they understand with blinding clarity that it doesn't get a whole lot better than a lilac bush with a butterfly on it."

   Diane and I don't have a lilac bush, but we do have a butterfly bush with hummingbirds working its blooms. Every so often the little twits swoop over when we're sitting in the yard and hover in midair just a few feet away, brazenly looking us over. Do you have some little things in your life that you're especially grateful for?

4. **Start a gratitude journal.** Dr. Emmons also says that focusing on gratitude leads to having more to be grateful for. He reports that psychological research now shows that putting positive thoughts into concrete language has advantages over just thinking the thoughts.

5. **Oh, my God!** Take time to thank God daily, no matter how you're feeling. I especially like to do this during my early morning meditation time. I usually begin by telling God, "Father, it's your son, Mike, down here in the war zone of Planet Earth, coming before Your throne of grace to thank You for another day of life." Other times I go to the Cross in my mind's eye and say to Jesus, "Thank You, thank You, thank You..." Doing that reminds me that I have an eternal future. It's a real depression buster, too.

Sometimes I thank God for loving me by quoting a sweet Scripture back to Him. For instance, I might begin with God's words: "I have loved you with an everlasting love. Therefore, with loving kindness have I drawn you"—Jeremiah 31:13. I reply, "I love You back, Lord. Thanks for loving me first and making it possible for me to love those around me, even my rebellious teenager."

And now a gratitude story. One recent December when he was 53 years old, attorney John Kralik felt as if he didn't have a lot to be thankful for. His small law firm was failing. He was struggling through a painful second divorce. His children had grown distant from him. He lived in a tiny apartment where he froze in the winter and baked in the summer. In addition, he was forty pounds overweight, and his girlfriend had just broken up with him.

Then, during a lonely hike on New Year's Day, John was struck by the belief that his life might become at least tolerable if, instead of focusing on what he didn't have, he could find some way to be grateful for what he had.

It all happened while he was walking in the Angeles National Forest above Pasadena. He was slightly lost in a growing darkness when he heard a voice that said, "Until you learn to be grateful for the things you have, you will not receive the things you want."

John pondered the message while sitting near the remains of an old hotel that had been destroyed by a fire and never rebuilt. As he pondered the message, he came up with an interesting idea: He would try to find one person to thank every day during the coming year. He would write a thank-you note. If he could pull it off by year's end, he would have written 365 thank-you's.

He took the idea seriously and began to handwrite thank-you's for gifts or kindnesses he'd received from loved ones, coworkers, and others—anyone he could think of who had done something nice for him, no matter how small.

He ended up with a small book entitled, *365 Thank You's: The Year a Simple Act of Daily Gratitude Changed My Life,* and I recommend it highly. Here are some of the anecdotes from his book. His first thank-you was to one of his sons for a coffee machine that brewed one cup of coffee at a time. The thank-you was short and sweet:

"Dear Son,

Thanks so much for the astonishing single-cup coffee maker. It's perfect for my office where we can offer everyone a different kind of coffee. Moreover I think my staff is a little tired of cleaning up the grounds and this is a very clean process. Nevertheless, I'm toying with the idea of keeping it for myself.

See you soon—Dad."

He had to call his son because he didn't know his address. After giving him his address, the son suggested maybe they could do lunch. They got together for lunch the next day, in fact. After making some small talk, he gave John a bulging business letter-size envelope. It was full of forty $100 bills—$4,000. "It's for the loan," he said. And that led to another thank-you note.

"Dear Son,

Thank you for paying back the loan. It was a great day for me because, actually, I really needed the money at this moment. More importantly, it built trust in our relationship. It showed me you were growing up as a man and that you could be true to your word. Love, Dad."

Thanking family and friends for Christmas presents resulted in ten thank-you's and left Kralik with 355 notes still to write. He asked himself if he really wanted to keep doing this.

"I might spend $146 in postage and countless hours writing notes, but where would I be?" he wondered. "Would I still be euphoric after losing my business or after a few other losses? If I died of a heart attack now, people would be wondering: What in the world happened to this

Transform Your Life With an Attitude of Gratitude • 57

guy? He was writing a lot of thank-you notes at the end for some reason—must have been lonely."

Then Kralik received a sweet thank-you note from his former girlfriend, Grace, for a Christmas gift he had given her. When he called to thank her, she told him she loved him and he decided to keep going. He wrote her a thank-you note:

"Dear Grace,

Thank you for the cologne. I now have confidence that I can smell exactly the way you want me to. More importantly, thank you for taking the risk of loving me at a time in my life when few would have dared. Your love is a treasure I did not expect to find, and often feel I don't deserve. Thank you for this priceless gift."—Love, John

Shortly after this exchange, Grace and John resumed their relationship. His life began changing in other ways as well, some of them subtle. By the end of February, when someone asked how he was doing, instead of complaining about his struggles he found himself reporting on things for which he was grateful, even if it was only making payroll that week or keeping his business open.

He started doing this unconsciously at first. But after he noticed what he was doing, he made the conscious decision to keep it up. So he began answering these kinds of questions by noting things for which he was grateful. He even caught himself using words such as *thankful* and *blessed*, though he wasn't a strong believer or church-goer.

Several hundred thank-you's along the way, John and Grace had their first real date at a baseball game. Two rows down, an elderly couple watched the game, and the man's wife reached into her purse and withdrew a sandwich lovingly wrapped in waxed paper. John and Grace were transfixed as the woman unfolded the sandwich and offered it to her husband. Then she adjusted the collar of his white cotton shirt, smoothed a few lumps in his thick gray hair, and whisked away a couple ticks of dandruff.

"Waxed paper," they said to each other. "Who does that anymore?" said Kralik. "Within a week both of us had bought rolls of waxed paper. I now wrap my daughter's lunch in it. If Grace stops by for lunch, she's wrapped our sandwiches in it."

He concludes, "You can give your love a nice house on the beach, or a Lexus, or even something bigger. But it won't beat a sandwich wrapped in waxed paper, or a thank-you note. Who does that any-more?"

By the end of his year of writing thank-you notes, John Kralik's entire life had changed. His law practice began to thrive, as did his relationships, even with former wives. About seven months into his new life of being grateful, he received a phone call from the governor's office. He had been appointed to be a judge on the Superior Court of the State of California.

John Kralik continues to write thank-you notes. One of his most recent was sent to his 8-year-old daughter and read like this:

"Dear Daughter,

Thank you so much for the brown tie with blue spots. It is just the kind of tie I like and it goes with my tan and my blue suits. It was fun to be with you over Christmas and New Year's.—Love, Dad."

He concludes in his book, "When I put on this tie today, I remember it was the gift that most brightened the end of my worst year. I wear it often."

Want to enhance your outlook on life, no matter what is going on? Want to see your life from a glass-half-full perspective instead of a glass-half-empty? Want to beat back the depression that afflicts you so many mornings? Hey,

Transform Your Life With an Attitude of Gratitude • 59

if you're not ready to write a year's worth of thank-you notes, consider this exercise which I wrote about earlier.

Start practicing being thankful for five things at the beginning of every new day. Thank God out loud for those five things or write them down. Then watch what happens. I think you'll be fascinated at the positive impact this little one-minute exercise will have on your mood.

"No matter what happens, always be thankful, for this is God's will for [those of us] who belong to Christ Jesus." "Rejoice in the Lord, always. And again I say Rejoice!"—1 Thessalonians 5:18; Philippians 4:4.

Come on, call out five things you're thankful for during the next minute! You can do this. And if you'll do it every day, the Holy Spirit will use this exercise to transform your life.

"The Holy Spirit will change you into a different person."
—I Samuel 10:6

EIGHT

Ransomed!

At 7:30 on the morning of September 23, 1994, Tom Hargrove, a business executive working in Cali, Colombia, to help the locals learn how to produce more food from their land, found himself in big trouble.

He was driving down a familiar stretch of the Pan American Highway, ten minutes from home, and was running a little late for work. To avoid traffic congestion, he took a fork in the road that looped back around to his office and went through the scenic countryside. Minutes later he encountered a roadblock. No big deal, he thought. Police and military roadblocks are common in Colombia.

But as he looked at the dozen or so young men surrounding him, bristling with M16s, AK47s, and a collection of 45- and 38-caliber revolvers and Che Guevara berets, his heart sank. He had survived three tours in Vietnam, and now he was going to die in Colombia, he thought. But that wasn't the case. Instead, he was being kidnapped by the Revolutionary Armed Forces of Colombia.

The next eighteen days passed without a word to the outside world from his kidnappers. Then came the first ransom demand—for $6 million. By that time, Hargrove was long gone, hidden away in the cold, forbidding Andes. His captors moved him constantly from one primitive mountain camp to another. He was so isolated that for the next eleven months he would not see a wheel, a road, a window with glass, or a fork or knife. Before his ordeal ended, he would lose fifty pounds and his hair would turn orange from malnutrition.

A diary he was able to keep revealed his state of mind after nearly eleven months as a captive: "Terrible despair, but must fight it somehow." And in another entry, "Can't allow deep despair like yesterday. Cry too much. Must stop." Two days later, "I will not go crazy." And several days after that, "Live today, only today."

Over the many months that dragged by, the $6 million ransom was negotiated down to $500,000 and paid; but no Tom. Then, at the end of month no. 11, in the words of his wife, "This very strange man walked into my bedroom, who smelled like ashes and had orange hair." Her Tom was home again.[25]

How much would you pay to ransom a loved one?

If it was a particularly troublesome family member—a difficult in-law or rebellious teenager—perhaps you might think about making the abductors pay you. But if it was someone you loved with all your heart, how much would you be willing to pay? A thousand dollars…a million dollars, if you had it…everything you owned?

Would you give your life to rescue them?

The Bible tells us that when Satan took our world hostage, Jesus Christ used the "R" word and said, "I will ran-

---

25. *The London Daily Mail* reported in December, 2014, that Colombia is the kidnap capital of the world even today

som them." Here is His own complete statement: "The Son of Man did not come to be served, but to serve, and to give His life a ransom for many"—Matthew 20:28.

When Satan deceived Adam and Eve into rebelling against God, he became the prince of our planet. Jesus used that very language. Everyone became infected with what I call Mad Cow Disease of the soul. Selfishness replaced selflessness. Self-love took the place of genuine love. And survival of the fittest became the norm, along with all the baggage of a satanic nature: deceitfulness, rebellion, immorality, dishonesty, and other such characteristics, resulting in death.

- God had only two ways to get the planet back and stop the infection.

- Wipe out Satan and the human race and start over. Or, the Creator Himself could pay the ransom, His death the price for saving you and me. Since God is love, He allowed Jesus to become one of us and so pay the fearful price our redemption required.

The Bible tells us that God "paid a full ransom for His people"—Psalm 111:19. The apostle Paul underscored the point when he wrote, "He is so rich in kindness that He purchased our freedom through the blood of His Son, and our sins are forgiven"—Ephesians 1:7.

So there you have it! Jesus died so you and I could become normal: loving, kind, gracious, and positive difference makers in the lives of others. Loving, kind and gracious are not normal traits for human beings. Some of us may fancy we're that way, but the Bible tells us that "the heart [human nature] is deceitful, above all things, and desperately corrupt, incurable"—Jeremiah 17:9.

Your primary news headlines within the past seven days should underscore this point! And if that doesn't work, reflect for a moment on someone who really took advantage of you along the way. Then consider the hateful, bitter (or other negative thoughts) that may well up within you when you remember the event.

To get another perspective on the price Jesus paid to ransom us, take a look at the amazing Being Jesus was in His glory.

If you've ever been temporarily blinded by the flash of the sun off a passing car, then you have a hint of what it's like to be in Jesus' glorified presence. When His old disciple John saw Jesus as Revelation 1:12-16 describes Him, he said, "His eyes were bright like flames of fire...and His face was as bright as the sun in all its brilliance."

And John fainted!

Other descriptions describing Heavenly beings refer to a body that looked like "a dazzling gem. From his face came flashes like lightning," and "His voice was like the roar of a crowd"—Revelation 4:3; Daniel 10:6.

With this celestial description of Him still in mind, consider that Jesus "did not consider equality with God something to be grasped, but made Himself nothing, taking the form of a servant" as He came to this planet.—Philippians 2:6.

How much lower can you go than to make yourself nothing? Well, perhaps lower still if you get turned into sin and are destroyed. The Bible says that God made Jesus "Who had no sin to be sin for us."[26] Then in an incomprehensible moment of both wonder and horror, He destroyed the sinful Being Jesus had agreed to become at the Cross when He took on our sins.

The Old Testament prophet, Isaiah, predicted this. "Surely He took up our infirmities and carried our sorrows, yet

---

26. "God made Him Who knew no sin to be sin for us so that in Him we might become the righteousness of God"—2 Cor. 5:21.

Ransomed! • 65

we considered Him *smitten by God, smitten by Him* and afflicted...and by His wounds we are healed"—Isaiah 53:4, 5 (emphasis mine).

Now you might ask, If God is love, why are people terrified and passing out in Jesus' glorified presence? The answer is the corruption of the human heart (think self-centered, immoral, deceitful, critical, violent, dishonest, rebellious, impatient, and mean. Why do you have to be so mean?)

Jesus' fiery presence either consumes these ugly traits or ultimately kills the person who chooses to retain them. To the pure in heart, His presence brings rejoicing. For the impure, it's pure hell. They can't get away fast enough. Of course, apart from Jesus, we're all corrupt "above all things,"[27] the Bible reminds us.

When time runs out on this planet—as it should soon—the apostle Paul tells us that "the Lord Jesus will be revealed from heaven with His mighty angels, in flaming fire..."—2 Thessalonians 1:7, 8. If a glorified Jesus showed up today where you are, which way would you be moving? Toward Him—or away from Him?

Those who have accepted Jesus' ransoming work at the Cross will have no problem with that fire. The Bible says they will receive new bodies that "will shine like the sun in their Father's Kingdom"—Matthew 13:43. However, those remaining in their corrupted earthly state will die. (Revelation 20:7-9).

By the way, Jesus' fiery presence also means protection for those who love Him. "When you walk through the fire," He tells us, "you will not be burned"—Isaiah 43:1-3. You likely know the story of Shadrach, Meshach, and Abednego who were thrown into a fiery furnace by ancient Babylon's

---

27. "The heart is deceitful above all things and desperately corrupt, incurable. Who can understand it?"—Jeremiah 17:9

King Nebuchadnezzar over their refusal to worship one of his false gods.

Jesus was with these guys in the furnace. Afterward, they walked out cool as cucumbers, not a hair on their heads singed (see Daniel 3 for the full story).

So powerful was the impact of that experience on Nebuchadnezzar that even though He obviously never knew the name of Jesus, he became a Christian 2,000 years before Jesus actually came here in the flesh. (Daniel 4:37).

God's ransomed followers have the same protection available today that those Jewish young men enjoyed. Let's say you're a person afraid to go out alone at night. May I suggest if you're ever confronted by the bad guys, you can tell them, *"In the name of Jesus Christ, back off!"* and they will have to fall back. Jesus' name exudes that kind of power. Heavenly fire power for those who've accepted the ransom He paid for those who trust Him. Jesus Himself reminds us, "Behold, I give you power...over all the power of the enemy"—Luke 10:19.

The Bible also tells us, "The name of the Lord is a strong fortress. The righteous run into it and are safe"—Proverbs 18:10. "The Lord will fight for you, and you have only to be still"—Exodus 14:14. Isn't it awesome that the One Who ransomed you on the Cross also promises to protect you wherever you are on earth and to even fight for you?

Jesus' name is far more powerful than any gun or pepper spray you might carry. So every morning, why not take the time to place your life within the name of the Lord and know you've got protection! You would be smart to start practicing those words now, so if you're ever confronted by dark forces, you'll have all the weaponry you'll ever need. Here they are again: "In the name of Jesus Christ, back off!"

Now let's switch gears! In your mind's eye, having

Ransomed! • 67

looked at Jesus in His glory, look at Him again, His divinity hidden, as He hangs naked on the Cross with nails in His hands and feet doing His ransoming work.

What an unbelievable comedown! The King of the Universe Who spoke 100 billion galaxies into existence, now stripped naked. *Why naked?* He's already been sucker punched, spit on, His back laid open with seventy-eight strokes of a lead-tipped whip, and nailed to a Cross. *So why naked*, for goodness sake?

Jesus goes naked so you'll never have to. The Bible tells us, "The time is coming when everything...that is secret will be made public"—Matthew 10:26. In other words, every awful thing you've ever done, but hoped no one would know, will be exposed. Except for those who've accepted Jesus' ransoming sacrifice of Himself. About them, He says, "I will remember their sin no more"—Jeremiah 31:34.

Jesus wants to have your back. He took on what otherwise would be your nightmare. Don't you just love Him for doing that?

If you accept Jesus Christ as your Savior today and every day, then that's your ongoing status with God—redeemed, ransomed!

Got any secret sins in your life? Don't cover them up for one more minute. Deal with them now. Jesus has ransomed you. He took on your sins at the Cross. So accept the ransom, His life sacrificed there instead of yours. What a deal!

Every ransom has a drop spot. Tom Hargrove's rescuers had to go to five different locations before they found the right spot to leave the half million dollars needed to ransom him. You and I need only to go the Cross every day and accept what He did for us right there.

By the way, real Christianity is a lot more than merely believing Jesus Christ is the Son of God and died for your sins. Receiving Jesus is just as essential as believing in Him. "But to all who received Him, who believed in His name, He gave the right to become children of God"—John 1:12, 13.

In your mind's eye, go to the foot of the Cross every morning and receive a spiritual heart transplant. The good news is that Jesus is in the Spiritual Heart Transplant business! It's His specialty! And He has promised, "I will give you a new heart and put within you a right Spirit"—Ezekiel 36:26.

Like a new heart today? Just ask. Jesus has prepaid one just for you, and the Holy Spirit installs them free for the asking every day. Why daily? Because as I've mentioned earlier, your old heart is always trying to make a comeback. The Bible tells us to "put off the old sinful nature [which] loves to do evil…and put on the new self, created to be like God in true righteousness and holiness"—Ephesians 4:22-24.

If this isn't a daily experience, you will drift back to what you used to be. The Bible says "your choices are never free from this conflict"—Galatians 5:17. Perhaps this is why Jesus told His prospective followers, "Whoever would follow Me, let him deny himself and take up his cross daily and follow Me"—Luke 9:23.

And now a final question! If you could go to the Cross with the knowledge you've just received, what might you say to Jesus?

Have you ever spoken to someone who was dying? I still remember flying from Portland to Grand Rapids, Michigan, a few years ago when my dad was dying. I got to the hospital just in time. Dad couldn't respond verbally when I got to him, but we made profound eye contact for a long minute or two. He gripped my hand hard as I told him I loved him. Then very slowly, he let go. A few minutes later he lost consciousness. Three days later, he slipped away.

That moment meant everything to me and, I think, to him. But Jesus didn't get that kind of break. No one said any I-love-you's to Jesus when He was dying. We are told that Jesus longed for a comforting word, but the closest He got was a request from a dying thief who had an "Oh-my-God" moment that Someone was right beside him Who could ransom him.

Perhaps you're having such a moment yourself. If you are, don't let the opportunity slip away. Jesus is right beside you right now, too, and He is telling you, "I stand at the door and knock..."

So why not tell Him, "Come in! You're welcome here. Please come in and give me a new heart. Put within me a right spirit, your Holy Spirit, and...change me into a different person"—Revelation 3:21; 1 Samuel 10:6.

But now back to the question, What might you or I say at the Cross if we realized it was the Creator of the universe[28] offering His life there to ransom us?

How about (saying these two words out loud and slowly), "Thank You, thank You, thank You, thank You...

"Thank You, thank You, thank You....

"My Savior and my God! Thank You!"

Do this every morning for a solid week, and I'll guarantee you one thing: You'll know without a doubt you've been ransomed—by the blood of the Lamb!

---

28. See John 1:1-12

"The Holy Spirit will change you into a different person."
—I Samuel 10:6

NINE

How to Experience God and Become a New You!

It is a standard plot in science fiction. An alien parasite infects the brain of a hapless victim and slowly converts its host into a slave before finally taking its life.

In nature, this horror story plays out every day in Costa Rica. The participants in this deadly drama? A parasitic wasp and a puppet spider.

In the opening scene, the wasp stings a puppet spider, paralyzing the spider—then it glues one of its eggs onto the spider's abdomen.

When the spider wakes up, it shakes off its grogginess and goes about its normal life. For a week or more, the spider constructs webs and catches prey. All the while, the spider seems unaware of its charge even as the larva drills holes into it and sucks its blood.

On the spider's final night, it suddenly starts spinning a

strange, oddly shaped web in response to a chemical the larva injects into the spider's blood.

Once done, the spider sits quietly in the center of the web. Within a half hour, it is dead, apparently poisoned by the larva. The larva then sucks the spider dry, discards its husk, and spins its own cocoon in the web that has been specially designed for its survival.

In a few days, a wasp emerges and flies off to find a mate. Then it returns, seeking fresh spider care for its young. So the cycle, which is very hard on the puppet spiders, continues to repeat itself.[29]

The world of humans is almost as horrifying as that of the puppet spider. The Bible says by being born here, we're all stung by a corrupted self. This self needs to be replaced daily.[30] Allowed to survive, it's our assurance that we ourselves won't survive, ultimately.

Most of us seem normal on the outside, but we're really damaged goods on the inside, often just waiting to explode or do something crazy. Psychiatrist M. Scott Peck wrote famously a few years ago, "Most of us are mentally ill to a greater or lesser degree."—*The Road Less Traveled*, p. 17.

Unless we deal with it, the demonic larva of our natural self will linger on the underbelly or our souls until it has slowly sucked the life out of us.

So our lives become quite a tangled web. The larva gives us brief highs and long lows. It sends us into denial and blinds us to the fact that life on this planet is dreadfully abnormal. Some examples:

---

29. "The Case of the Puppet Spiders," *Los Angeles Times*, Oct. 26, 2000, by Usha Lee McFarling.
30. "If anyone would follow Me, let him deny himself and take up his cross daily and follow Me."-Luke 9:23. Why daily? Because our old self is always trying for a comeback!

- The person who seems normal but is a rageaholic behind closed doors.
- Or she who refuses to give up a habit or addiction with the caveat: "I know this is killing me, but we've all got to die of something."
- Of course, the capable, the self-sufficient, the brilliant, are so hard to help until some terrible moment brings them down. And over time it always seems to, doesn't it?
- And for so many there is a thought life corrupted by bitterness, rage, fear, hate, and their many cousins.

Every so often we try to make positive changes, but rarely see them through while our self-larva clings to us, keeping us numb, and riding us all the way to oblivion.

To all who are in such a condition—and we all start out that way—the Bible offers only one answer: Look at your Creator! Look at Jesus! Jesus? Jesus who? Jesus Christ, the Lamb of God Who paid a full ransom so you can obtain your freedom. He knows you're paralyzed. He understands you may be entangled in the world's web. But if you will look at Him, He will rescue you. And transform you.

Makes no sense, you say! Well, consider this true story. When the Israelites in Bible times were attacked by poisonous snakes (likely the deadly sand vipers of the Sinai desert) enroute to the Promised Land (Numbers 21), victims were dying in almost every tent because anti-venom serum hadn't been invented yet. However, God said if those who were snakebit would just look at an artificial snake, the act of looking would be their antidote.

What an irrational idea! Except for one thing. It worked! Every snakebit person who looked at the artificial snake became well.

Now the ancient Israelites may have dimly understood

that the snake was a symbol of Satan and their sinful selves. But they likely had no idea that the snake was also a symbol of the Messiah Who would appear 2,000 years into the future and pay the price for their rebellion. But you and I can know because Jesus has already come and ransomed us, as noted in the previous chapter.

It's by looking back to Jesus Christ our Creator that you can find healing today.[31] In your mind's eye, look at Him right now in human form hanging on a Cross carrying your sins and diseases.[32] As the end approaches, see Him panting out His life there, fighting for every breath, and know that you weren't bought cheap. The Bible tells us He "paid a full ransom" to save you and me from annihilation.—Psalm 111:9.

Also, when you look to Jesus on the Cross, realize that Jesus didn't just die and return to life in three days. He died what the Bible calls the second death (Revelation 20) which is eternal loss of existence. When your sins and mine were placed on Him, Jesus endured the horror of second-death hopelessness that the unsaved will endure one day even though He was resurrected.

Your life will be transformed if you will look at Jesus at the beginning of every day. The light of His countenance shining on you will have a catastrophic effect on Satan's larva. So no matter how hopeless your life may seem to be, keep looking. Just make eye contact and welcome Him into your life. He says, "I stand at the door and knock, open the door and I will come in and we will share a meal together"—Revelation 3:20. Invite Him in!

Invite Him in, and your corrupted natural self will become overwhelmed by your new supernatural self. Pursue

---

31. "He created everything that is. Nothing exists that He didn't make."—John 1:3
32. "He took up our infirmities and carried our diseases."—Matthew 8:17

How to Experience God and Become a New You! • 75

this experience daily, and Jesus, through the Holy Spirit, will give you a new self, created to be like Him. As you experience His love, you will be filled with all the fullness of God.[33]

So now you have a decision to make. Perhaps you're motivated to look to Jesus, but you're thinking about the high you will lose from whatever has you. Just remember every high has its price and behind every selfish indulgence, depression awaits you with a snarl. A depressed friend of mine recently referred to that experience as "the hell going on inside my head."

We all have two choices. Let our natural self live on, make choices that intoxicate but never satisfy, and over time slide down the slippery slope of numbness, depression, and death. Or we can look to Jesus and receive the fruitage of a relationship with Him: love, peace, patience and immortality. Indeed, He promises to give you "all the desires of your heart" –Psalm 37:4. What a deal!

You may continue hearing of the Middle East terrorist group called ISIS that often murders its victims by beheading them. In Jesus' case, it wasn't a knife that took His life. Scripture says it was a winepress that killed Him.

Ancient winepresses consisted of two planks brought together by a third which crushed the juice out of the grapes. The Bible tells us that figuratively, our sins were the winepress that crushed out Jesus' life on the Cross. It was on the Cross where God the Father separated His sustaining presence from the Son in His humanity. Jesus went through hell there so you don't ever have to.

Similarly, the unsaved will experience their own hell when Jesus returns in glory. The Bible says, "They will see His face and will call for the mountains to fall on them"—

---
33. "And to know the love of Christ which surpasses knowledge, that you may be filled with all the fullness of God."—Ephesians 3:19

Revelation 6:16. They will do anything to get away from Jesus' face on that day when "every eye will see Him"—Revelation 1:7.

Why such a horrific response? Because they will have permitted the larva to remain too long! That's why the Bible instructs us to "put off your old self, which is being corrupted by its evil desires, and to put on the new self, created to be like God" every day.—Ephesians 4:22-24.

Those who choose to retain their natural self will have missed their healing time. Now the nightmare of their eternal loss is about to begin.

However, you and I need never know that experience. Because Jesus tells us, "Look—I've engraved you on the palms of My hands. Turn to Me and be saved."

So when you hear the words, "Look, the lamb of God Who takes away the sin of the world," take a good look. You'll be transformed!—John 1:29.

Now here we are the end of this book, with many of us finding ourselves in circumstances not unlike that of the puppet spider and parasitic wasp.

Once upon a time, you came into this world full of yourself, with a demonic larva attached to the soft underbelly of your soul. You didn't know what was going on, perhaps not until this moment. But the larva (your natural self) did its devastating work just as the parasitic wasp infected the puppet spider.

But now you know! Now you can recover! Because Jesus tells you, I know you're paralyzed, so just look at Me and let Me into your life. "The Holy Spirit will come upon you in power...and change you into a different person"—1 Samuel 10:6.

How do I look at Jesus? you may ask. Well, one way is that Jesus inhabits His promises. You can look at Him and find Him in them again and again. Perhaps with promises such as these:

"'You will seek Me and find Me when you search for me with all your heart. I will be found by you,' says the Lord"—Jeremiah 29:13, 14.

The Lord says,

"I will betroth you to Myself forever; betroth you to Myself in lawful wedlock with unfailing devotion and love. I will betroth you to Myself to have and to hold, and you shall know the Lord."—Hosea 2:19, 20, Moffat.

Look at Jesus. It's your first step toward becoming a new you.[34]

Let Him into your life every morning before you do anything else, and He will transform you into a positive difference maker in the lives of those around you. At the same time, He will prepare you for His soon return in the clouds of glory.

---

34. To deepen that relationship, review the checklist in Chapters 3 and 4 every day.

"The Holy Spirit will change you into a different person."
—I Samuel 10:6

TEN

HOW TO KNOW YOU'RE GOING TO HEAVEN

SOME GOOD NEWS FROM THE BIBLE.

1. God's message to you: **"I have loved you with an everlasting love"**—Jeremiah 31:3.
2. Your natural state: **"All have sinned [rebelled] and fall short of the glory of God"**—Romans 3:23.
3. The result of remaining in your natural state: **"The wages of sin is death, but the gift of God is eternal life through Christ Jesus."**—Romans 6:23. When the Bible uses the term *death,* it means eternal loss of existence. When it uses the term *gift,* it means that eternal life can never be earned by our good deeds, only received.
4. **"But to all who *received* Him, who *believed* in His Name, He gave the right to become children of God"**—John 1:12.
5. "He Himself bore our sins in His body on the tree,

that we might die to sin and live to righteousness, by His wounds you have been healed"—1 Peter 2:24. Jesus paid the price for our sins on the Cross. Then He defeated death when God the Father resurrected Him. Because Jesus defeated death, in Him, you can too.—2 Corinthians 5:21.

6. **"For God so loved the world that He gave His only son that whoever believes in Him should not perish, but have everlasting life"**—John 3:16.

7. **God gave His only Son to our planet forever.** Among the planets and other life forms among the known 100 billion galaxies in the universe, Jesus will always be identified with Planet Earth. He gave up Who He was in Heaven to become the God-Man so that we can become Sons and Daughters of God, heirs of God, co-heirs with Jesus of the universe, and live with Him forever.

8. **"You must be born again."**—John 3:3. In order to be born again, we have to die every day to our human nature, exchanging it for a divine nature. Ephesians 4:22-24 tells us to "put off your old self which is being corrupted by its deceitful desires...and put on the new self created to be like God in true righteousness and holiness." When we accept Jesus Christ as our Savior and Lord, the Holy Spirit makes this transaction a reality. In Ezekiel 36:26, He puts it this way:

9. **"I will give you a new heart and put a new Spirit in you.** I will remove your heart of stone and give you a heart of flesh. And I will...move you to follow My decrees and be careful to keep My laws."—NIV

Three Wonderful Promises

"And this is the testimony that God has given us eternal life; and this life is in His Son. He who has the Son has life; he who has not the Son of God has not life. I write these things to you who believe in the name of the Son of God that you may know that you have eternal life"—1 John 5:11-13.

The Bible says, **"This is the secret: Christ lives in you"**—Colossians 1:27.

Jesus says, **"I stand at the door and knock; if anyone opens the door, I will come in..."**—Revelation 3:20.

Let Him in right now, won't you?[35]

---

35. Don't I have to keep God's Ten Commandments to be saved? Commandment keeping won't save you. Keeping them is simply the evidence that you have a saving relationship with Jesus Christ. Hebrews 8:10 and Revelation 14:12 explains what we do and what God does during our journey.

ADDITIONAL CHAPTERS not included here appear in a longer version of this book entitled

Snakebit: We're all snakebit
also by Mike Jones, M.A.

Available at: Amazon.com

For special pricing on bulk orders of 10 or more, contact the author at mjonespdx1@gmail.com.

If you enjoyed this book, and would like to write a positive review on its Amazon page, the author would be grateful!

Made in the USA
Charleston, SC
16 January 2016